ANIMAL ANCESTORS

Written and illustrated by Jon Hughes

Contents

Collins

ANIMALS FROM ANOTHER TIME

Can you imagine a world with horses the size of small dogs, whales that walk and birds three metres tall? They all lived on Earth at some time in the last 60 million years. They are now extinct but their relatives live on – and you'll probably know them very well!

Fossils like this tell us what the ancestors of today's animals looked like.

In this book you'll find out about some amazing animal ancestors from long ago. You'll also find out about their closest living relatives. There is a size guide on each page showing the animal ancestor next to an adult human. You may be surprised by the size of the animals!

Can you guess what the ancestors of these animals looked like?

THE IN-BETWEEN DOG

or *Amphicyonid (say: am-fee-sy-on-id)*

Another name for the in-between dog is the bear-dog, because it's an ancestor of both bears and dogs. Bear-dogs lived across Asia and North America until about nine million years ago.

Scientists have found footprint fossils which show that the bear-dog walked like bears do now. It moved its two left legs together first, then the two right legs.

The bear-dog lived in underground dens and fed on smaller animals. It was a strong digger and could burrow after its prey.

closest living relatives: bear and dog

4

How big was it?

THE ARGENTINE BIRD

or Argentavis (say: ar-jen-tay-vis)

The remains of this huge bird were found in Argentina, in South America. It lived there until about five million years ago.

It was the largest ever flying bird. It was 1.5 metres high, with wings that measured 7.5 metres across. Each wing feather could be as long as 1.5 metres.

This ancient bird ate small animals such as lizards, mice and rabbits. It also ate fish.

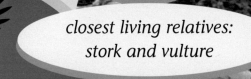

closest living relatives: stork and vulture

How big was it?

THE INDRIK BEAST

or *Indricotherium (say: in-drik-oh-theer-ee-um)*

This animal lived in Asia about 30 million years ago. It was the largest ever mammal to walk on land.

The very biggest of these creatures grew to about 4.5 metres high. It had a long neck that made it even taller, so that it could reach leaves high up in the trees.

It was also a very heavy animal. A really big one weighed 15,000 kilograms – that's much heavier than the largest rhino!

closest living relative: rhinoceros

How big was it?

THE EARTH MOLE

or Mammoth (say: mam-oth)

People used to believe that this animal was a giant which lived underground and died when it saw daylight. But we know now that the mammoth was a type of large elephant.

The bones of mammoths have often been found half-buried in frozen parts of the world, but in fact they lived in many different places. Those that lived in cold countries had long fur to keep them warm.

Mammoths grew up to three metres high and ate mostly grass and bushes. They had two long tusks which they used to protect themselves from attackers.

closest living relative: elephant

How big was it?

THE MIDDLE HORSE

or Mesohippus (say: mess-oh-hip-us)

About 40 million years ago, this small, dog-sized animal grew to look like a little horse. But unlike a horse, it didn't have hoofs on its feet. Instead, it had three toes on each foot.

It was only about 52 centimetres high, but it had long legs. This meant that it could run fast and escape from sabre-toothed cats and other meat-eating animals.

This shy little animal ate only fruit and leaves.

closest living relative:
horse

12

How big was it?

THE PAKISTAN WHALE

or *Pakicetus* (say: pak-ee-see-tus)

Fossils of this animal have been found in Pakistan. They are 54 million years old.

This ancient creature is an ancestor of the whale. It had legs rather than flippers, so it could walk on land. It also had nostrils at the end of its snout, rather than a blowhole on the top of its head.

This animal was a meat-eater and probably hunted fish and other small mammals that lived in or near to water.

closest living relative: whale

How big was it?

THE GIANT SHORT-FACED KANGAROO

or *Procoptodon (say: proh-kop-toe-don)*

This animal lived in Australia until about 50,000 years ago. It weighed up to 200 kilograms – that's more than twice as heavy as today's biggest kangaroo.

Each of the creature's hind feet had one single large claw, like a hoof. Its long arms could stretch up over its head and its long, grabbing "fingers" could reach leaves high up on trees. It was able to chew really tough leaves with its strong jaw.

closest living relative: kangaroo

How big was it?

THE SABRE TOOTH

or *Smilodon (say: smy-loh-don)*

Another name for the smilodon is the sabre-toothed cat. Many well-preserved fossil skeletons of these creatures have been found in California, USA.

The sabre-toothed cat was very fierce. It had two long, sword-shaped teeth which it used to kill its prey. It could open its mouth very wide – almost twice as wide as a lion.

It had short, sturdy legs and a very short tail. It couldn't run very fast so it probably hid, then pounced on its prey.

closest living relative: lion

How big was it?

THE TERROR BIRD

or *Titanis (say: tee-tarn-is)*

This giant bird lived about two million years ago in North America. It couldn't fly because it didn't have wings, but it did have arms covered in feathers.

This bird stood nearly three metres high and could run very fast. It was a meat-eater and hunted small animals, using sharp claws and a very large beak to grip and kill them.

closest living relative: moorhen

How big was it?

ANIMAL ANCESTORS

walked like a bear	largest ever flying bird	had a long neck	had fur to keep it warm	only 52cm high
lived in an underground den	ate small animals	weighed 15,000kg	had tusks to protect it	ate fruit and leaves

could walk
on land

had a long claw
on each hind foot

had two long teeth

couldn't fly

was a meat-eater

had long fingers

had short
sturdy legs

ate small animals

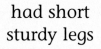

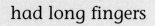

Ideas for guided reading

Learning objectives: pose questions prior to reading non-fiction to find answers; scan a text to find specific sections, skim-read title, contents page etc, to find out what a book may be about, make simple notes from non-fiction texts; build new words from reading linked to particular topics; work effectively in groups by ensuring each group member takes a turn, challenging, supporting and moving on

Curriculum links: Science: variation, plants and animals in the local environment

Interest words: ancestor, amphicyonid, argentavis, Indrik beast, mammoth, mesohippus, pakicetus, procoptodon, smilodon, titanis

Word count: 964

Resources: small whiteboard and pen

Getting started

This book may be read over two sessions.

- Show the children the book and ask a volunteer to read the title and blurb. Support reading of the word *ancestor* and discuss its meaning.

- Ask the group to skim-read and say what the book is about. *What is the animal on the cover and which animal of today is it related to? Do they know any other animals that lived a long time ago?*

- Model how to choose an animal ancestor from the contents page, turn to the relevant page, read out the text and information, and summarise the text in a few facts on the whiteboard.

- Ask the children to choose their own animal ancestor from the contents page. Explain that they will be repeating your modelling: finding the page, reading the text and information, and writing down what they find out.